The Songs That Objects Would Sing

poems by

Roxi Power

Finishing Line Press
Georgetown, Kentucky

The Songs That Objects Would Sing

Copyright © 2023 by Roxi Power
ISBN 979-8-88838-330-8 First Edition
All rights reserved under International and Pan-American Copyright Conventions. No part of this book may be reproduced in any manner whatsoever without written permission from the publisher, except in the case of brief quotations embodied in critical articles and reviews.

Publisher: Leah Huete de Maines
Editor: Christen Kincaid
Cover Art: Sky Power, *Passing Through*, 2022
Author Photo: Marcia Quackenbush
Cover Design: Mary Gilliana

Order online: www.finishinglinepress.com
also available on amazon.com

Author inquiries and mail orders:
Finishing Line Press
P. O. Box 1626
Georgetown, Kentucky 40324
U. S. A.

Table of Contents

I. The Mute Acceptance of Objects to Receive Our Fragment-Song

Tracking the Lost Nerve 1
The Songs that Objects Would Sing 2
The Mind of One Rose 10
Arrows of Thanatos 14
Not Here 15
Blood Moon 16
Hives of Fire 18
A Song Was Lit 19
A Very Fragile Radio Wave 20
Brick Patio 21
West Texas Thanks You 22
Pumpjacks 23
Uniform 24
Name Outlasting Name 25
Desert 27
Odd Return 28

II. Unpaint a Landscape

Implying a Trip to Wyoming 31
Capitalism is Dying Inside Us 34
Stove Prairie 35
Zig Zag 36
Fresh Wildflowers 37
Pandemic Getaway 38
There's a Ruin Inside of Everything 39
Ghost-Scratchings 40
The Aftermath of Future 43
Evidence 44
Catharsis 45
We Start so Many Parties by Accident 46
A Real Theater of Crisis 47
Contact Tracing 48
Unsaid, Unseen 49
They Say 50
Soaked by the Story 51

III. If We Are Our Own Ruins

If We Are Our Own Ruins 55
Sitting on a Deck Chair at William Jones' House
    in Felton, California 56
I Saw a Bird, and it Wasn't Even Real 57
In the Time Between Your Fingers 58
The Hole Sits Pretty Waiting for Us 59
Portals 60
Thanksgiving 62
Smoke Progressions 63
Driving that Road to New York to See You 64
Both And 66
Painting by Porchlight 68
Seawall 69
Waiting It Out 70
Rummage 71
Differentia 72
If You Spoke 75
How Did We Find Each Other? 76
White Noise 77
Why the Song Cannot be Sung 78

IV. You Are a Found Object

Inland from Beyond 81
One Place or Another 82
You Are a Found Object 83
Synthetic Realism, or Myths about the Fall 84
Storm Trilogy 85
Crooked Heart 87
There to Protect the Song 88
Vagrant Hummingbird 89
The Music that Never Ends 90
Desire Blows the Dust off the World 91

Acknowledgments 92
About the Author 93

*For my daughter, Emma Joy,
and all the ancestors who came before*

I.

The Mute Acceptance of Objects to Receive Our Fragment-Song

Tracking the Lost Nerve

A call and response to Miles' Davis' "Saeta" from Sketches of Spain

I.

A roll of presence infiltrated by scratch and origin
Ominous horizon unfolding in rhythm

One voice solitary cracks the blue surface of twilight
A piercing of matador vocabulary. Militant but troubled
troubadour neighboring the pink beginning of the solo

His voice the cry of wilderness inside a graph of obligation
Everywhere you listen, a jangle of broken and reconstituted
memories, fairly new to this aperture. They came, they cried
and they left, leaving regiment in their wake

II.

That old urn of loss. Against the night of your absence,
one trumpet plays. Its voice a crisp green pear
hanging on the last tree

In the unseen mountains, yellow cymbals shake
on aspens, still clinging, rhizomatically connected
in a forest, a family. Still intact

On trumpet days, I feel your paper-thin hand holding
mine, pulling me into a forest I meant to visit when you
came long ago. Now we sing of this as though it's myth

Resurrection only happens when we resurface
after a long sleep in ocean's twilight. Truth flares—
an electric blue iris after the last winter rain

Grace. That old note, that old snatch of song that takes
you there will return and return. Though you will not

The Songs That Objects Would Sing

for my Mom, Iris

Imprints of the other world
   Stalks of yearning keen in the wind
      connect down there to
         something
They dry out above but whistle
    a familiar but never-heard
  tune   Blue streaks on the petals
    of night inflict us on our own drift
for beauty   A line down the middle
  of the dream says this diptych is safe
to watch   but do not cross
   Elemental drives pull us there
      against our will but
not so far   I'll speed along
          in this lane, long as I can

      Mortar inflicts a sense of placement,
  a there that's always been.
Mixing & shaping & placing of bricks
  all forgotten once mortared.
    They are just there as though
they always have been
    a place for the mind to rest,
escape the panic of space

We were there together
  in a placement against all odds
What do we really know about starting
    from scratch?   In a bed, in a belly,
  in a bardo?
      No "I" there yet but reaching—
Samsaric portal. "Countless aeons"?
    Better breathe & forget about it.

So I had you for a lifetime
           & now cannot imagine what next.
Read a book about what happens? Subscribe
         to a theory about how we'll meet again.
   Tired of all who pretend to know.

I feel you in the glint of objects sometimes. That's all I
   know. That shimmer down the length
of spider web, that omniscience in the chandelier
      unseen til now but for a flickering instant—something.
    All is projection & mind play? "I need you" or "stay!"
       & the brass goes back to being
just brass. If I let "you" watch "me" & loosen
  the grasp, I may see a twinkling
         again, who knows.

———————————

       If I say I can't stop, perhaps I'll just
keep going past parentheses, brackets,
    all manner of punctuation & transitional
    phrases, into horizon, infinity's coda.
If I say I can't stay here & finally footnote
myself off the page, will I know where
     to find the book where once
         I was a chapter.

Right now the view is anthology view—
    a grove of leaves. Through my window, vertical
   green and brown. Redwood trunks, thick & high,
block the sky. Foliate womb
          makes infinity cozy.

———————————

    I would commit to elegy except
the sonorous trickle of stream teases
    the mind back to a cusp whereon

        we launch our gratitude for options.
          The sound that dust makes as it coalesces
into star?   My dog's great ears pick up
        insect rattle & leaf stir. And somewhere
someone hears those tiny yellow flowers
      sing themselves toward tomato's green beads.
        So is death, then, no song? Elegy fills
the absence, to soften fear's follicles, just
            poking through.

———————

To say to my young daughter, watch or listen
        if you want to know what life is—
is to say life is anxiety. Dog leaping
    toward bird sound, bird leaping
        from dog sound. Who sits absorbed,
      inside sound's centerless, edgeless surround?

If I could paint the so-called absence
  of sound—Cage's silence—its impossibility,
       stemming from Rauschenberg's white paintings,
there would still be the hum, the heartbeat, quiet
      but not silent.

So there are sounds that stand in for
     you. "Some strange music
drags me in." Just now it's "dream a little dream
of me." I see your knowing smile, hear
your voice swing. Is this what the living do?
     Dream little dreams for those who cannot?

———————

   Drawn deep into creek side locutions, I trust
this continuity whose music cannot be
    rehearsed. Improvisation with certain stationary

      facts. A rock here & here with this rushet
of water will likely make this tone.
Last night's rain, a phenomenon of air meeting air
         like smiling strangers in a crosswalk—
some thunder that passes, but leaves behind tomorrow's
      new song.

The creek song is different, yet the same.
   Same rocks tune different water until
     it lulls me to a forgetfulness
Nietzsche said would heal. Looking
       back, to better times, to Monumental
   History, when your Mother was alive.
        Or looking back like Orpheus:
"Forever"—an extension
      of the present moment & what is
        not there.

To relate with you directly,
    a photo propped up by red birdhouse
  your wistful garden of a smile
        the last my eye recorded
           as you lay dying

I was not yet a warrior, & am not,
      mostly.
  "The world does not end," says
    a poet, and I say
which world?

    When I held you, as you lay
dying, when you died, when I
     held you, in my arms, I had a
   glimpse of the warrior we all are
       buried beneath the dream of
         permanence.

        I'd never seen such a beautiful face,
yours. Steady in the moment that contains
   the entire past of it. All that was
 not. The depth of it drowns the book
         & can only be etched in bone
    or the stories that others will tell

Prismatic life. Hold it up to the light, there is not one,
    but many. When all things coalesce, when each
  strand retains its own. The path between earth
         and heaven painted by the messenger,
 Iris.
         And yet, to describe it is, as Keats said,
    "to clip an Angel's wings," to "unweave a rainbow."

    Seven colors like seven notes in a scale from hot
to beyond deep blue. "Mood Indigo," you used to play.
   Your favorite song, and your sister's too.
   You'd play until it sparkled baroque,
and then you'd dance it   blue.

   Oh Mom, those fingers curved over my hand.
I can feel your skin, too tight over bones,
     like leather gloves left out to dry
after a rainstorm. The piano you thumped, until it turned
  into story. Then the fingers dried up from disuse.

   And yet to see them, fragile & beautiful—pink
     half-moon fingernails—artist's hands lying over
my own, is to sense beginnings & to have a song
       I could play one day.

    The shame of beauty: it doesn't know
it will not last forever. Its eyes grow sad as it
   sees this, then ripen, underground,
 into jewel-colored yams that will feed
   one of us one day.

What will burnish the song to amber, frozen
                ember of all we ever were?
It was just a moment—
    but it's what   we have.

———————————

Each leaf has a light side
        & a dark side. Each life,
    a mirror for the sun, & a shade
        for the dark forest floor.
                Each leaf, a story
            that once was not there
                & will not be, again. We see
the leaf & think it's there, its
    thereness comes from being there
now. Paltry imagination.
        Places where winter's memory
is summer's goad, help us to write
        the real, not the wished for,
                story of the leaf.

Here the leaves are green & green & green
            without end & I can be fooled
        into thinking it was impossible
                that you died.

———————————

            Stiff little moment. How to dance you
    into pliancy—admiring that grandfather redwood
            preceded & will outlast me,
                witness to a storm.

            Neurosis of Steller's Jay—its matrix shriek
    going out in all directions from a single
            point: an asterisk of sound, no
apperception there.

Who are the inward-focused here?
        The cochineal among such racket-makers?
    Dipping inside to bear witness to one's own
                wells.

The light now is an inner light—
      patches of remnant sun on logs
          deep in the forest floor seem to
      radiate from within. Equinox
around the bend, soft illuminated surround
    mocked by the jay's razor tail cutting
    up the oak leaves with its angry switching.
           my branch *my* branch *my* branch

    How to reenter the conversation
  with objects that bear your subtle
signature, your cinematic fictions
          I sew from scratch—in this
    song-strafed foliate mosh pit.

———————————

And so we undulate in time
   you there, me here. Orphan twine.
      A moon curtained by rain.   Inside
we're framed by sullen window shades
  while sultry emerald leaves drip
     future from the other side of the pane.

If I hold my end up this side
  of the pane, can you rest
  folded in eternal thought?
The counterbalance to forgetting is
   frottage   an apparition of what once
     was there, rubbed back into likeness
enough to help us see what is no
      longer there

———————————

When I touch the objects
          that bring you to mind
touch upon them, when I touch
     your dust? your crumbs?—
               when I—

          like an archaeology of closed eyelids
               candles once lit and frozen
          the angel's lips open in a song
            she is about to, but has never
  & never will
                         sing—

          the mute acceptance of objects
               to receive our fragment-song
a circle free of dust once we
               lift, and by lifting, enter
     the story
               replacing the clean halo
with a mess of fictions
          that startle us back to grace

Rapt, we listen to what
                never was & will be again

The Mind of One Rose

for Cleo

    revisit the room   outside
                              where you,

        ambient fog

hover   just off the   sharded

   shore   fog horn

         bellows in the   rose

  its tight folds   turn crimson as quiet

     scream   deepens   to color

we long for   you   are

    everywhere   as thought is

          running like the bird fountain
through levels
               in a loop

  it looks   like   plenitude

        someone fills it   unseen
  each day

the birds   don't   know

    cracked motors   white

   butterflies   dance around

      red-tipped jade

a squid garden　　　of aloe

　　balms　　　　　for the day

　　　　without　your
　　　　　　　　　　phone call

　　there is　　　your　　　　name

and stories　　with　　　　gaps

　　　like a
　　　　　missing
　　　　　　　　step

　　　　　on the　　　staircase

you　crying　　　　on　the
　　　　　　　　　　　　landing

　　language　and　　thought

shattered　　　into　　　shards

　　　beautiful　and　　terrifying　　but

　　in　a　　　　　　Modernist　　way

　　　　the listener　filling in

　　　fragment-song　　with　　meaning

love　　　　　　longing
　　　　　　horror　　　　sorrow

where then is
　　　　　the fog
　　　　　　　　　　　to soak
　　the succulents　　　　　　the pumpkins

       the mind's dried   rinds

  waiting for the Nietzschean   fog
                                    of forgetfulness

               the Keatsian   mist
                                of   remembrance

    that are   themselves   and/or
                     that are   metaphor

     the rose and its   screaming heart

needs   or absorbs   our projections

          a darkened theater   co-opts

the   day   like the compressed
             gallery
                   in your   skull

  project lightning forks   molten orbs

on its walls   as you   need

        the stems of you
                branches of you
                           petals of you

grow now in the mind's   garden   various

    as grieving   is

plots are seeded   or   ceded

    by chance   mostly

       baby birds in the   lemon tree

                bring us back

sharpen senses   rather

    than   entering   into

                  the mind of one
                                      rose

and its   unheard
                     spiral   tightening

      over emptiness   like a baby's

                        fist

Arrows of Thanatos

The aim of life is death. Sigmund Freud

The shortest route to
quiescence, down the stairs
of October, to hasten what
has begun. I wrote, "I need
to get to New York," and
why, in otherwise sprightly
buds at dharma center in
August, I saw fossilized
nerve endings and thought
"Cleo." No reason, yet.
Cried, tried to make art of it
when I needed to make
haste. Arrows shot from my
mind to yours but feet
fossilized on the ground
where I practiced talking to
God like the Rabbi taught us.
It required walking, and I
found the shortest route to you
planted as reminder, to always
act on what you are given to know.
The shortest path to you now
is prayer. This poem and all others—
flakes of rust, memory's minerals—
I offer as advance on the ticket
that's already bought.

Not Here

Sometimes when I want to talk to someone
about how you're gone and will never return,
I want to talk to you. You would understand.
You would say, oh darling, you want me to
come over? Let me make you dinner.
I want to tell you all about this hole
where you were and how it's too big
and yet too small to contain your star light.
But I've fallen into it and lost the map
to the rim, a wound I circle. I'd rather stand
in sublime terror at the edge than watch you
shrink into a scar that could fit on my hand.
Deft reminder of impermanence,
how we carry trunks of china and photos
of ancestors with us into imagined eternity.
Already, my daughter is getting rid of everything.
Even the perfect storage space beneath
her bed is empty as if to warn me
those boxes of all of us won't make it
to the other side of any canyon.

I think you'd prefer it this way. To let you
go rather than to tumble in after you
brought down in the stretch between
that last moment your eyes held mine
and the time when you returned,
eyeless, in the urn. To be no longer held
in your regard, what's left is to hold you
the way you'd want. A long kiss, looking
into my eyes—as if you meant to burn yourself
into me—before you ran from the cab
to Grand Central to catch the train
that would take you away for good.

Blood Moon

for Liza

Morphine fogs the city
She lies behind the horizon now
A hill full of the watchful waiting
at the crest of Dolores Park
for the eclipse. "Where's the moon?"
the children cry. Loving voyeurs,
gawking at what is not there
Is that what death is like?
One heaven or one face
may hide another

You lie in bed, waiting
for one short sleep past
this pain. Everyone
watching you like TV
A deep draw might clear
things up—this morphine fog,
this lung gravel

There was a time in June
when the irises came out
We'd dance in our silk slips
inside gardens. We felled
the stalks too soon, scattered
them in the empty room and
spun, legs flying up the walls,
jazz burning in our hips

We are growing thick now
on the hillside. Nodules
cluster in lungs, spread each
moment. Looking for the rare
red moon. Little girl in a red velvet
dress in a slow-motion slide down
the hill. "If you want to see a red

moon—that's it." Blood moon,
sky wound, something missing
in advance

Hives of Fire

There's a pointedness to this indirection
I'd like to flow against, or not, to places
or moods untasted since we sat in the poetry
chairs by your woodstove, and into the hive
of time we melted like honey-comb candles
whose windows grew wider. Light fell through
them, opening to pasts lying like coats
tossed on chairs, the last thing he wore before
leaving this realm.

Yet the imprint of living went on past the clearing
of clothes and the chairs in the bedroom he left
for the last time, now sold with the house
that may still hold them, like spirits, who knows.
I can return, since I still have my memory,
unlike my father in his last year.

The songs that these objects still sing
are sirens that beckon backwards,
dare us to step with naked feet on rocks,
pin points of memory's allure.

Now, in your room of tea cups and books
blankets and candles, and old Russian
harps, I can breathe and write
like a late autumn fire contained
in its stove. Wood turns to smoke,
to dance and to fireleap, but bottled
like dreams that shift in mind's chambers,
lighting the hive, contained like a night.

A Song Was Lit

The flame of the candle endures
  reflected in the black of your deep
      piano, hovering above
    a note as if a tulip head
  rooted to sound, stems unplayed
    in the dirt of possibility.
A song was lit in the making
   of the moment, each petal growing
    or falling, all the while
       something like song and
something like light filled
         the inky silence.

Outside, crickets still sang, rubbing
   their legs against the cold
of October. We knew to enter
     this song before the steam pots
   of January rattled on the stove top,
    reminding us that music of a sort
     will always come through
  in tones or timbres that shake
against the force of their making.

  How do we stand upright, ready
    to be played? Symbols shake loose
     from Emily's mind when all we have
  left is Eternity—something she glimpsed.
    We conjugate and conspire
with ancestors, their words full
  with their own preemptive absence,
unknowing then that it could all be
      lost in a symbol, a sound.

A Very Fragile Radio Wave

All I have is your hummingbird letter-opener, broken now
by clumsy misuse, then oversignified to amplify the gap
between the living and the dead.

I leave this room of objects that bind me to the broken.
Swerve around plots of American flags, private sidewalks
of guarded eyes, fencing in what is theirs on the 4th of July.

Repair to the garden of my friend. Anna's Hummingbirds,
your favorite, tussle for the blue hydrangea. Everything
returns me to you, a very fragile radio wave I tune into now.

Radio Free You—if I'm lucky. Streaming beyond punctuated
time of life, death. To feel the emptiness, you need the form.
And when the form is gone—

I need new guises to remind me how to talk to what is missing
as though it's not, conjure a continuum of plenty without
resorting to spiritual procrastination. "See you in heaven?" etc.

We scribble poems as planes strafe the redwoods, compete
with monster truck song. Further afield, the cement-white
skies of Lincoln Plaza, rigor mortis with black jets.

Words fly across shadows on our pages. My finger,
ringed by the turquoise you left, curls around the pen
that writes toward you as you recede.

One hummingbird is made whole by the flowering
maple. We brush against our own signals
and listen for further instructions.

Brick Patio

Tomatoes ripen on the sill. Bright green
   light mingles with the live things you
with careful early morning hands
      snap, stem, husk, then toss
into fresh shapes, discrete yet blending,
   fit to scoop. Words topple. You spark
   kitchen talk, we spin the carousel for sugar,
pepper, plum preserves. Concentric intimacy.
   Round oak table where we sit for hours
     spinning into years. Dominoes shuffled
after supper. Tiles laid out between still hands
   and flighty ones. Impermanence as ritual.

Pipe smoke and rose musk shelter
   the warm brick air. His pipe packed roomy.
     Copper green chair glows at the edge
of the dark plains. A light haze of crude
   pulled up by nearby pumpjacks spreads itself
   among locust hum. Fireflies blink, cats rustle
beneath bushes. Peaches bend boughs,
     heat lightning at dusk. Prospect
of distant storms. Smoke script,
a long love letter beyond the caprock
   to West Texas stars above the brick patio.

How you lay the foundation by hand
     in the sand, no cement. A woman's
masonry builds rooms with no ceilings,
     infinite solitude. No laws but
the spiraling logic of breath.

West Texas Thanks You

It's as if somebody is sitting in the lawn chair
watching us from childhood. He smokes
his pipe in the dusk, and it spirals up
through cricket song to the stars. We call them
West Texas stars, but we don't own them
despite ourselves. We call them omens
and sisters and evidence of history.
Millions of years later, here they are.

If I watch my breath, will it know? It once
seemed natural, like the rocking chair
and all the stories it heard without trying.
She lives through my scrapbooks during
the pandemic. Somebody sometime
got to be 13. Did you touch each other?
Guffaw up each others' noses? The eternal
pose of happiness. I frame this soliloquy
with reminders that you don't get to bare
midriffs 40 years later. The '70s were different.
Now a geological museum of stories warning
how a kiss can derail a family.

The serious thing is still waiting in that chair,
the iron one with the empty heart. I can see
a teenage thistle through its hole. Everything
dances together from 1963 to the unknown end
of the song even if you can't hear the tune.

Her door closes again and you think latches are
so symbolic. A satisfactory click-click and for now
you can put up your pole and give the catfish
a break. West Texas thanks you for stopping by
however briefly on your way to wherever
you were never meant to go.

Pumpjacks

On a long dank train through Texas, she
    told the curious her name was Steve.
Long brown curls stuffed into a woolen
        driver's cap.
Her grandmother warned her she'd go bald
    someday, grounded her to her seat & said
 little girls are never named Steve.

Outside, pumpjacks swayed like anemone
    & she dreamed of going home. In a conflux
of thrust & gravity, in a perfect rhythm
  upon their fulcrums, they seemed to be drawing
from a hidden river. Sluiced to the train
     they pumped it south. Long lonely whistle
and the bittersweet, oil slick night. The cotton
   just poking through.

   Stark black arms rocking up and down,
  up and down. They made strange
     the sudden sighting on crests of cottonwoods.
Eerie displacement into yellow smell.
       Stars burning & breathing the sulfurous night,
the earth's arteries thrumming in the long shuddered ride.

    The smell was sweet & with the oil came
the expectation of that strange arrival. Midnight.
  Streets wet. The lights of the Piggly Wiggly would glow
soft & the refinery condense the night scent,
    lilac, sulfur, and peaches. The Sinclair dinosaur burned
in the sky, spinning on an axis above her.

Uniform

The cowboy hats, driver's caps, baseball caps
you bought me in the Kmart of your divorce.
As if in losing our family you might succeed
in gaining a son. The Texas ranch owner
you'd worked for sent boxes of velvet dresses.
Mom, after all, wanted to name me Missy.

By second grade, I managed both versions of
myself, tackling girl-magnet Jim, during recess.
A pile of girls nearly kissed him to death
until he neatly ordered us into days of the week.
I was Wednesday. As the harem and school holiday
rules pushed me back into the box of dresses,
I made a compact to wear lumberjack boots
with holiday dresses. Few were amused.

Tackled Jim in front of the second-grade teacher.
Just hugging. But she grabbed my ear,
marched me to the front of class, warning all:
"Little boys can beat up little boys. Little girls—never."
The boys still let me play football with them,
sometimes even quarterback.

Dad's blue Toronado pulled up at recess.
He'd driven from Texas to Wyoming with a uniform:
shoulder pads, helmet, everything. Managed
to get it into my hands before my stepfather
herded him out of town. Something about not
paying child support. To me, he was just dad.
Both dads were okay with tomboy me, but only
one could saddle me with his last name.

Name Outlasting Name

I
Oh father Father
 name I never swore
lips inform the ears
  parting lips for the word
       a closure
your cry the cry of chainsaw
  hidden as stuck trees
 stones thrown like words
conspire a cathedral of stones
  I bring the awl, the paint at night
   for graffiti and small fractures

to unconstrue the structure of a name
 to by degrees deny
 mere degree?
printed tongue and stepping stone
  step-father your name is
       undone

II
your name is besides
      although
          until
  design a name to spin off
  the shelf
saucers china or ice
      eclipse one word   spell it after
      splice word one
to the center of the page
      in the unbought book
  between is a matter
of espionage   "my name"
  erased by the text

III
sword of the Other
  in the father corner
your arms lift me
  like strong documents
  into a separate name
with a separate syllable
        yours
rustling of integers under
  my ribs   a bond
for repaying
your name is
        dust-flies-riled in the tracks
        buyer of islands off Belize
        lake of Wyoming leaping with trout

you would venture in Wives and Daughters
    I would shape if to shape
    to spin the lie
  like pearls to grit
elbows buried in the scrupled heap
  and deciding to pass through fire
        or fire again

I paint my name on a palette of egg shell
  unprimed

IV
this might not have to do with you

Desert

Living on the swollen edges
  of my father's heart sutures
these last weeks, I think of my
  sisters. When shall
we three meet again? All of us gone,
      who will rub the balm
on his chest? From this prop plane
enflamed canyons turn to pink dust.
  His sutures were much straighter
though. These are many fathoms deep.
  As we close in, I can see his were no less.
    Stubble on this land. His chest, bare,
baby smooth. A rock stomach and the sagging
  breasts of a grandma. This seventy year old
man afraid and refusing to show it.
  Feeling marked by an angel or the blinking
eye of God, awakened after a lifelong siesta,
      prompted by something as accidental
        as an ant bite.
      Oh Father, we want to make ourselves light
      as the glint of light off the spinning
prop. To enter a photon, hushed.

Odd Return

I'm writing letters to you in advance
of your leaving, like another beginning beneath
the beginning. One we think we can't discover.

Swainson's thrush song spirals into wind
without beginning, blows acorns on our tin roof
making the earth sound like it's cracking.
I hear the timer ticking like there's only so many
lines left. How many, did you say?

I miss you, my sister, and you're not even gone.
Don't worry, you say. You'll make an odd return
to where you never meant to leave. We can
find our way back from the woods where we may
yet be eaten by our own alienated labor.

Pretty sure that's what the witch in my dreams
after Dad left kept trying to tell me. She waved
goodbye at the end of the driveway. Her hand
was a rake, displacing Dad's mower.
Time to clean up all that's dead and fallen.
Her disturbing little smile held a secret.

Fifty years later, I returned to drop off ashes
of too many of us in the cement planter
at the end of the driveway where the witch stood
because it screamed urn and irresolution.
Witches apparently never die unless you
stop remembering them.

And the red clock keeps ticking toward
the same ending we all write toward
even if we go there at different speeds.

II.

Unpaint a Landscape

Implying a Trip to Wyoming

All that matters is a ghost
or the traces of memory left by event in
the event we get lost inside
the kindness of mind's occasional
remembrance of this moment, this.
Not the other who keeps scratching

      *   *   *

Implying a trip to Wyoming is not the same.

      *   *   *

Has anyone ever been to Wyoming?
Don't answer this time.

      *   *   *

A stretch of Wyoming that I found repeated:
bald, opinionated rocks.
A multicultural train set
chipped red, blue, & yellow
squandering Rawlins across the night.

      *   *   *

Polysemous star factory:
The mind's light rail shedding no regrets
as it trucks steady through the panoramic voids
studded with granite cathedrals where
the parishioners pass in Peterbilts,
and we dream of antelope leaping
but never over fences, and snow
drifting towards us from the other side
of the story.

      *   *   *

Jauntily, Wyoming spreads its future
across the black veins in the cretaceous outcrops.
The hemisphere holds its breath,

glances down at its shoes, while Cheney's teeth
prepare to rip the skin off Wyoming. And sutures await us.
Have we had too much to sleep?

Somewhere uranium gives you
that "come hither" look and you whisper god.

*   *   *

Jaundiced July. Make-up artist
of the meadow, behold. Below this amber crust,
veins throbbing with hot history unwritten.

*   *   *

Beneath each rock, a vein.
Each vein, a pipe.
That drive over here?
Permanent, fatal. A hollow we can't pack,
a stolen era, stripped.
Wyoming, please say
something.

*   *   *

>   Batter my heart, three-personed sky
>   wind (objectifies me)
>   blue (cuts my eye)
>   curved space (visible theory on Interstate 80)

For there is no home to "go back to."
There was only always this risible
sky, fond of no expression in poetry,
only the brush,
sometimes on Hurley's canvasses.

*   *   *

Am I permitted often to return
to this sky framed like a meadow
in the lens? Aperture grasps
and hurls the blue meadow
onto the back of the mind, emulsified
into a place to stand inside and outside of.
You can't "use" your environment for poetry
a poet said.

*   *   *

Are there ages when we are between ages,
stammering toward, but arrival never arrives
When all is the hiss of highway and
a soundtrack that empties the narrative

This place where memory and scenery fold
like a hinge you solder
from scratch. How to make the two
make it swing?

*   *   *

Where there was driving
there seemed too much Wyoming.
Apace with eternity, this an assault
on boundaries, all. Unchanged too.
No jar placed on a hill, no object
to quicken or distill. Just the fact
of wind and clouds ever arriving.

Capitalism is Dying Inside Us

Stepping into a car dealership. "Just looking."
What would it feel like to drive that
on some empty highway that never existed?
Two hours later your mind is gray powder.
You dare to yawn at the sales rep, 6pm on a Friday.
"Have to meet my friends for dinner. Haven't seen them
in a month." I was on a road trip in Wyoming,
crowded with the fantasy of emptiness.
"Would you rather eat dinner or get the deal
I will never give you again?" Something dies
in me as I walk out.

Even I-80, Wyoming, a town of 12 people
every 100 miles, is wall-to-wall with semis
carrying t-shirts, air fryers, press-on nails to Walmarts.
If you pass one in a Prius with California plates,
they box you in, like you're stealing their elections
or manhood.

Another fantasy, McConaghey's hand light
on a Lincoln wheel as he sets out alone
on the long twilit road called Texas.

Stove Prairie

Colorado High Park Fire flames over mountain,
rolls like tsunami toward Stove Prairie Ranch
200 yards away. Billy loads the horses in an hour.
Her boss in the mansion hands her a broom.
"Put out the flames by my favorite birch."
After a few minutes beating the ground, she turns,
"Please get in the Jeep." Panicked Sheriff arrives
with orders. Old woman burned to death in her house
up the road. Stallion, kicking for the mare in heat,
won't leave. Billy rides Mo, a gelding ridden only
a few times—as green as they get—down Buckhorn
Canyon. Evacuation traffic, flames lapping.
The photo—legendary.

A month later, shadows stripe along green prairie.
Charred trees hover by fence. Horses, returned
refugees, swish tails by broken hay bales.
Ground squirrels take over, dig tunnels that menace
the Morgans' ankles. Stove Prairie somehow untouched.
Whole mountains will lie stillborn in moon ash for decades.
Shifting wind made a "dirty fire," burned in blotches,
zig zagging across random trunks, tree tops, leaving
killer trees—dead, but standing. Evidence of what was,
like a cemetery. The too-green grass between ruins
unreal, lit from within by phosphorescent bones.

What is luck? Hawk feasted on rodents left behind.
Evacuees smoldered in rumors the prairie had burned.
Among miracles, the unloaded filly and mare among
embers in an unburnt patch, circled by blackened trees.
Some make it by dumb luck. Others through a grace
they think they know. I know only Mo stands in a pool
of glowing hay. There's plenty of fuel left in these forests.
And it may yet rain tomorrow.

Zig Zag

Just last week, in the Wind River Mountains of Wyoming,
settling back into the dustbin of the bygone. Smelling the roots
of childhood's cheatgrass, long grown past advisable memory,
when your call came from California. "Mama, please come."
15 minutes to decide what to pack. The fire half a mile from our door.

The forests of California, almost all of them, ablaze.
A thousand lightning strikes in the dearth of August, and
fire season rushed in like a sudden relative unannounced
and spreading. I sped toward you through the Tetons
like a cartoon flipbook, then the wide bottom of Idaho, snaking
riverside until opening onto the last chasm, open heart surgery
of light in Twin Falls. Beyond, all darkness and disconnection.
Phones don't ring in Nevada. Until morning in Elko, that
clanging mirage, halfway home from anywhere. Particulate
hope formed a barrier between sleep and escape. Then your call.
"Turn back, it's useless. It's a long, smoky burn, nothing to be done."

Tried to take the measure of my instincts after a sleepless night
of cheap motel, bleached midnight of COVID. Turned against
my grain back into the circus of semis, I-80 East, toward Salt Lake
and whatever could hold me next, as our house stood shaky on
the edge of the Lightning Complex Fire. Ashes in urns stood still
on shelves, as the fire zigged and I zagged, along the long
Bonneville Salt Flat day, speeding to the next makeshift home.

Bonneville put me in mind of Bonny Doon, homes nested in
the redwoods west of us where suddenly friends were posting,
"Our home is gone." There is nothing west of Salt Lake but salt.
Nothing to burn that hasn't already, millions of years before,
and mineralized in the marrow of unknowable memory, minds
long sifted back in smoke to stars and watching us all,
we love to think, in times like these.

Fresh Wildflowers

Brought north to my senses, tears dried to mica.
Granite outcrops of emigrant stay. Running
from California fires back home.

Angus frolick, unaware of the future,
graze on fresh wildflowers, bursting
with nutrients seeded from clouds.

Crunch of tires in red dirt, then silence.
A present pregnant with pines,
welcoming as ranch wives or fuel,
arms spread skyward in a gesture of plenty.

Glance up to plural blue. Slate, aqua, steel.
Round nimbus tips slide like drips
of a Pollock into Medicine Bows.
Mountains just a thicker dab of dusk.

Tie Siding neighbor, Galvin's ex, Jorie,
admonished us, as young poets, not to use
our environment for poetry. Follow Stevens'
"cry of the occasion" through alluvial digressions
back to the source of the cry. Home, the final
source and destination. I always return here—
Cherokee Park, Colorado—as I would to my
grandparents. Lines etched into granite faces.
Protective, enduring.

Back in California, shallow root balls
smolder unseen in the night.
We return home, wherever we are.

Pandemic Getaway

Focus on the three horses,
heads down, chewing on a wet
summer of grass, on the same plane
as if posing for the painting. My sister:
"I don't paint from photographs but
the feeling from memory."
You paint wide stripes of vista,
like pastel Rothkos of Wyoming sage,
Texas caprock, Cape Cod dunes.

This summer, you said your favorite
place was the road to Jackson Hole.
Tetons with an attitude now muted
by the Dixie Fire almost 1000 miles
away. Smudged painting we hope
to restore. Turn up the AC, squint
at ghostly silhouettes that poke
through a basin of smoke.
Collects remainders of California
as if a reminder: no escape.

Stir our coffee with plastic straws.
Pull over to look at the last bison
shrouded in haze and hydrophobic gray.
Long line of cars blow smoke up each
others' escape plans. Watch through
windshield like it's a bad TV show we hope
won't get renewed. Sigh at the odds.

Entitled to smoke in the mountains of late
capitalism. Masks optional as Delta variant
takes flight, fells friends in Wyoming, airlifted
out of denial then back after dodging
death somehow. "I'm fine."

There's a Ruin Inside of Everything

Wild turkeys peck in the too-green grass
like the bright weeds after Hiroshima.
We park at the edge of burn, to witness.
The forest stretches thickly, drawing
a circle of grim roulette around our chimneys
still surrounded by walls and lives. Unlike
that stark gray finger on the hill, reminder
of the random riffs that create epic in their wake.

The air is a sludge of silence.
There's a ruin inside of everything, burning
in secret, singeing the edges of sound.
A dozen wild turkeys, black wattles swaying,
cross the road to the next ruin. Almost
New Year. Our minds, green fields
we walk, safe from the sirens. For now,
just peering inside the gutted black
mailbox fallen from its perch.

That side of the road, unsooted white
picket. This side, burnt out hulls of sedan,
flame-roasted coils beneath seats
stuffed with redwood duff. Cars slow
around curves taking in loss like news
footage. The untouched house perched
on the edge, witness to its own dumb luck.
Tan oaks' ghosted leaves, like late fall in upstate
New York before everything turns to nerve endings.

Ash sprinkled like snow or dustings of fresh
blessings on hoods of hollowed-out trucks.
But not. Stacked poles of old growth line
the highway, into new ruins. Soon, they say,
debris slides. After the parch, the cure
is the poison. Homage is not enough.

Ghost-Scratchings

i.
there is a candle inside of everything
asking to be lit

ii.
leaves, the color of white flame,
quiver on the precipice of winter

iii.
we were sisters, in an envelope of time
inventing language, hands clasped
around a column of wax, lighting the edge
of New Year, suspended in prayer

iv.
forever—feels that way when
the wick is lit and the mind
fastened to it with another mind

v.
but the color of that moon slice
the night you died was also ghostly
flame, lying on its back, unable
to spread in the frozen sky

vi.
a year and a half later, the forests
lit in an orchestra of flame
11,000 lightning strikes, 8543 acres
532 buildings, 214 homes
numberless pale leaves

vii.
what is that wan color that stutters
through the mountains now?
A beige lampshade, a stretch
of pie crust, a length of torso

caucasian in its insistence
to take over the visible

viii.
like near-death, and somehow
clinging, reminders the end can
linger, unpaint a landscape.
de Kooning's gesso, ghost-scratchings
through yesterday's paint: the spared
red barn and blue car on a hillside

ix.
disturbing light peach, crisp oval
remainders in dried flower arrangements
mom took to making after the divorce

x.
mixed with the smell of cigarette
clinging to each shag yarn
a beige house redolent with decades
remembered the span of a smoke

xi.
a shrine to better days
unopened on gold marble
precious lilac soaps fading
never to be frothed

xii.
we could light the tall cream
tapers, and they could dance
slightly in the mirror

xiii.
contained flame tip is like memory
something live on the stem
of nostalgia that melts us
slowly without ravage

xiv.
yesterday wasn't that
cement foundations with bronzed
rods like stalwart stems
promising to hold things up,
things no longer there, sizzled
into the past

xv.
the unhoused return to remember
their cream walls full of photographs
now a thickness of toxic sod
that may flow like history down hillsides
come January rain

The Aftermath of Future

The aftermath of fire bends time. The physics of fear disturbs
the mind. And yet, if I give in to this October afternoon's perfect
air quality, after last week's brittle skies, then do I relinquish
readiness and return to remorse at things becoming different
from what they are? Uphill, the man who never stops building,
seems to be screwing brads into steel. Everyone readying
themselves for the next stage—of what?

Why nest in further between these wires, interlaced with crackling
oaks? One just toppled into a week of blackout, reminding us
that "power" is evanescent, a privilege we should no longer build
around. Electricity, uncontained in lightning, connects us.

I may be here now with the plum tree brushing our roof, but put in calls
to tree trimmers. "Now" is just one fold in the snake-skin of time.
Three embers blown that way could spell an afternoon very different
from the one where I sit at a table rather than behind my wheel.

Next to me, *Frankenstein*. I spend the fall paging through Victor's
trauma, electrifying a life he couldn't care for. My students and I explore
galvanic concepts of life, sparks you can't control once unleashed.

Just last night I felt a substream of a life beneath this one that continues
like a parallel river below the one where I watch my family laughing
behind the window. In that river, our love continues from its first spark
and we live out some version of its unfolding, an alternate reality, "as if."

As I drove the 5000 miles of evacuation, friends spoke of quantum
physics: the past, present, and future happening at once. I try not
to live in the past, though I pay homage with scatterings of ash into rivers
across our childhood stories. The same river flows into knowable
future happening already, these friends say. I wouldn't know.
But probability scars the mountainsides, a zagging, illegible script.

Evidence

Same haze from multiple fires in Colorado
soften the outlines of Phantom Canyon.
No snowpack melt, no rain in this baked bone
of a state. Fires bring brome weed and yarrow,
pig grass and cheatgrass into glowing green relief
against the smoke.

Vista stepback from the fire that burned
our redwood valley a year ago. Sat atop
this same atoll, turning the Medicine Bow
Mountains into metaphor.

Think of the 60s, half-century slice of anger.
Pulling up every drop of crude. Culture wars
burn steady, a refinery flame. Now explode
in the Big Lie.

Strophe and antistrophe of fire dance across
any stage now, a chorus telling us the story
of ourselves across one short generation.

We knew in the 80s. Now we know we knew.
Exxon-Mobile records locked away
so they could offer us freedom of mobility
in exchange for a shrug.

Chorus isn't wise so much as angry.
Slept away a half-century of hope.
How we look when we teach each other
new refrains of Extinction Blues.

I want to learn all the names of wildflowers
surrounding me. I want to say at least I tried.

Catharsis

The subterranean time beneath
the time we spend on the surface
of things is where we meet sometimes
in a cave of indwelling. Wonder and
commiseration, soup and wine,
nourishment for all that is breaking.

Teeth, like leaders, cracking but not
quite ready to be crowned. Hopes
for the Swainson's thrush song
looping upward into an eternity
of grandchildren, though 50% of species
extinct within the last few decades.
Catharus, their genus, slants toward
catharsis, putting a heavy load of our
mental health on remaining songbirds.

If we are in the cave of aeon where
the linear rush toward omni-extinction
is hushed or stilled even for this one
story, then we live forever, we tell ourselves,
in this woodstove-warmed sitting room,
whatever losses await us.

We Start so Many Parties by Accident

Shelley felt herself the creature
responsible for her mother's death,
though she didn't ask to be that demon.
"I never *asked* to be born!" we all scream.
But now that we're all here, all 8 billion
of us…

Shall we seek revenge on our thoughtless
progenitors? Ok, Boomer. Now what?
Do you not owe me the same portion
of happiness you took? A mate, a job,
an oxygen mask? We start so many
parties by accident. Ways to avoid loneliness.
To not look at the shimmer of red maple leaves
before they fall to the ground in a storm
of wet endings. The lilac blooms for a week.
The cherry blossoms, clichéically short,
though a new metaphor is needed now
that they bloom in January.

If we stop spreading ourselves
like seed bombs across the graying
crust of everything, we could tend
to those creatures here now. We
invest in immortality when these drops
of rain, these birds—half of them gone
forever—fly in our sky *now*. Miracles
that took forever.

A Real Theater of Crisis

She visits like a messenger
from last year's normalcy
   tiny brown Anna's hummingbird
    tasting from the copper-budded
 troughs of the freshly-cleaned
feeder, here and gone
      like an apparition.
Now, the bees reclaim the nectar
  buds, more deserving of refuge
     than any of us, I mutter,
melting in August's anthropocenic
   sun. From this liminal perch
   between the so-called solid
past and the dissolving future,
    nothing is known. We wait
  for cues from the darkened
     wings where an invisible
  stage manager taps us
when it's our time in this
    endurance "happening."
  Inside this forest, where still
     trees seem to have all the time
  in the world, awaiting a worthy
line, there is a real theater
    of crisis. Roots brittle
from drought. Redwoods fall
  more often on rooftops now.
In live theater, Artaud said, we
     could die on stage. In fact,
  we are. Each word, a mortal
    gesture, dies
as it hits the air.

Contact Tracing

My sense of proximity to you
and your breath depends upon
your proximity to the world
and its sheddings. Contact
tracing would put a kink
in the cord that connects us,
so I just find space and hold it.

Early COVID questions. Can we
sit maskless in the yard two feet away?
Exhalations as you talk about no job.
If I pop on my mask—a kink in the cord.
I stay present for your story. Visible
trumps invisible. I can't see ACE2
receptors in vascular system taking you
in, hiding you, replicating you, inflaming
the walls of everything, so I just watch
the fear in your eyes, your future.
The understory of my arhythmic
heart gets louder as you talk.

Relieved when you leave. The curve
isn't flattening. Even as our cravings
for the chronic lawless days of summer
spike, and our muscle memory pulls
us out of chartered lives, another
muscle contracts, pulls us back
to secret chambers where we learn
about loss preemptively. We let
ourselves eddy on the surface of this
day, knowing it will end, yet knowing
it's part of a story that goes on
long after this one ends.

Unsaid, Unseen

I'm fleeing the screen, I'm fleeing
the scene. Friends perform "family"
on Facebook. I tip my hat, tip my hand
with cool daughter tricks, recitals.
"How grown up!" Slog through
reptile gardens of news: wearing
a mask = Democrat = worse than death.

People fall over on front pages. Nurses'
masked faces in hands, break down,
quick heart stab, swipe, no funding for schools
that don't open, swipe, must disclose his taxes,
but not before election, swipe, smiling families
wedge onto beaches like Cubist quartets
playing on the Titanic, swipe, cheek by jowl
in red hats at Tulsa rally, swipe, B&B
in Salt Lake on our way to Colorado!, swipe,
half the population has no jobs, swipe, swipe,
40% of deaths in nursing homes, swipe,
protesters against police violence pepper-sprayed,
swipe, if the last 5 Presidents were a "Karen,"
swipe, do you like my Van Gogh mask?, swipe,
canceled trip to Barcelona, frowny face emoji,
swipe, unamused cat: "when are you going back
to work, Karen?", swipe, Facebook memory
5 years ago: high school reunion when we could
still laugh open-mouthed, daughter won't let me
post her anymore, swipe, swipe, swipe, swipe.

What has been swiped? Are you tired yet?
Fired yet? Fleeing the screen, the scene.
Why aren't they posting? Maybe they're sick,
sick, sick.

They Say

What is this live wire
through my jaw, coiling
at the base of my neck
searching for a ground
at the end of my spine?
How do flowers make
their way through
the undifferentiated chaos
of green foliage to figure
so precisely, pink on the top
of an unlikely stem, as though
there all along? Was the journey
as excruciating as I fear?
I know it doesn't "just happen."
There is a mystery and a letting
go, like parenting a teen. You read,
select soils, prune, pray.
You remember your grandmother's
garden and hope for all that.
You remember Dylan's force and
green fuse and try to unclench
your jaw. Then it happens.
Or it doesn't. And it's nobody's
fault or credit, they say.
They say.

Soaked by the Story

Grief is the other face of praise you said as we
sat edgeward by the river, wanting to feel what
could swallow us. Here, everything was on its way.
Leaves, seed pods, foam, migrating south
on the surface, same pace but socially distanced.

Like us, on the surface of things, not touching,
not diving. The river is yet too still to pull us under.
We need a storm to let go into this wash.

If virus is a language, what is it telling us? We are too
many. Disconnected even before. But grief demands
obedience. River keeps marching toward moving shores.

Pathogens with a plan and a social network set up camp
under our noses then enter when we close our eyes.
They constellate like dust forming the idea of a galaxy.
Someone may see it from afar one day, like history,
and abstract our clotted lives into clarity.

We let go, like twigs into the flow, then dissimulate
like everything else until it's normal—too normal.
Everything moving on, dissolving without drama.
Numbers in the news. Some we know, lone trees
in myopic forests that fell us.

For now, we are forced to buzzing convents
to repent the waste, as our children flatten into
flickering panes. For her dance class on screen,
my daughter pulls elegy from her bones.
Both grandparents gone, without a goodbye.
She rolls, slow tsunami over couch onto floor,
soaked by the story.

III.

If We Are Our Own Ruins

If We Are Our Own Ruins

If we are our own ruins,
let's celebrate our gritty prominence,
letting the sun expose the cracks
that nobody tries to fix.

If we are designating the recent past
and almost future as a preserve,
let's at least not bomb it, like
the Alexandrian Library, out of spite.
If we are, in fact, ruined before we
step out the back door, swinging open
to our childhood summers, now but a
figment in the acid rain of news in our
late-Capitalist nights, then let's
reconstruct a bridge in the likeness
of these pocked visages and crumbled
arcs, a fragile stepway of burnt trees
and fire-cracked rocks, back to
a beginning we rewrite.

Face what we've made and will again
with stony-faced grace. Or say screw that
then dance among the ruins of ourselves.
Walk weavingly, Aristotle wannabes,
piecing together a path toward
happiness beneath the fallen rocks,
even for the crawlingest among us.

However we choose our attitude
among such remains, let's choose one,
and build some fine new cairns we need
not sign, "Rocky was here," etc.

Sitting on a Deck Chair at William Jones' House in Felton, California

Over my head, I see the bronzing leaves creep around the dying oak
stillborn like a pupa unfallen.
Across the ravine beyond our hidden house,
chainsaws outdo one another
into the scissored heat of noon.
In a criss-cross of light and shadow between redwoods,
a red-crowned hummingbird zags
within feet of my face, eyeing me.
I lean back as it zooms in like a drone with a package
      of unwritten poems.
It comes daily, unwritten, to the scarlet feeder.
I have wasted our summer.

I Saw a Bird, and it Wasn't Even Real

Lovers buzz-sawed about the bottle of nectar
hanging from the wrought iron sparrow.
Lovers or predators? Beloved or prey?
Hummingbird blurs between plum tree
and feeder, flaunts his raspberry chainmail
like a dandy or indentured knight. And
after reading Mary Oliver on "the third self"—
the creative mind we cultivate like a Medieval
knight, ready for any uncertain adventure,
because consciousness thrives on the unknown—
I no longer just think about indentured knighthood
as a metaphor for contingent academic labor. And that
thought indeed is a spear into the heart of Romantic
poetry, the mind that Oliver said sips on "Eternity."

And the mind that sips on paternity—the randy
hummingbird boy knows well. Has nothing to do
with parenting. And this might be a better metaphor
for the creative process. After the spark of genius
has embedded itself in an Other whom you feed
and steer gently toward their own destination
unknown to you both—except where fleeting "arrivals"
are recorded—something like a poem, a book,
or a person is permitted to stand on its own
as if its essence made this arrival inevitable.
Remembering the emptiness of form, we take
the measure of a self or poem, a baby bird or sutra,
and try to remember the random couplings—
a body and a chair, a journal and a pen,
a season and a tree—that sparked these accidents
of selfhood. They flashed forth and will dissolve
into crumbs of dirt and bone, parts of greater stories,
always unwritten in their writing yet again.
I saw a bird, and it wasn't even real.

In the Time Between Your Fingers

In the time between your fingers, a nest
of possible birds. They fly or evolve in the time it takes
to summon them since sprouting on this singular hand.
How handy they have been called to grade papers
for a legion who never wanted to write in the first place.

In the time between this regret and the next one,
you could have jumped into an undiscovered lake,
glacier-fed with pristine memories visible to the granite
bottom of the unlikely childhood, a kettle of fictions
fried up like the trout you caught on a line each time you cast there.

In the time between the time it took to winch yourself up the roadless
mountain to the lake, the lake has disappeared, replaced with a memory
of the lake that can siphon the air right out of the lung
if you leap. But there is always more air there in the time between
the words darting silently and uncaught in its cold and instant depths.

You circle the time between these leaps inventing the moves
you'd made up your mind to make sometime, clarifying
their depths and trajectories past known buried boulders
quantified in dusty topo maps, rolled up like ancient scrolls
in the backs of rare book stores. Sometimes you do this.

Other times, you stare out the window of everything you know,
the world framed by this portal that never moves, that is "yours,"
and the only thing moving is the rocking chair on your porch,
the wind moving it back and forth, never quite starting
yet never quite stopping for long.

The Hole Sits Pretty, Waiting for Us

There's a hole inside of everything worth knowing,
worth climbing inside sometimes, and other times
gazing into from the rim. The giant hole burned into
the redwood tree that my daughter, now too tall
to walk inside, used to run into alone, but only after
grabbing my hand a dozen times and making me duck
into this scary-fun doorway with her.

Getting to know the shadowy places, befriending
the concavities where creatures who we never
choose to befriend, choose to dwell—the spiders
who lay their traps, the rodents who build their nests—
until the children chase them out with gleeful shrieks.
"Let's go inside the tree" should always be our mantra.
Just now, 5 children calling each other scaredy cat crushed
in with parents as we sat outside writing. Did the tree
absorb them, as we absorb them into our poems?

They emerge. Object lessons in exploring hollowed out
histories or futures, making it an excursion. Pirate gems
of bravery. Like last night, when I asked your mom whether
she minded that it was a man who got her ready for bed
each night in her assisted living home. "I'd prefer a woman.
But I don't want to feel like a failure." We walk into the hole
holding any hand sometimes. "Is that wrong?" she asked.
"Of course not. Your bravery is moving, but you have choices."

For now anyway, it feels like there are choices, and
I guess that's what it means to be sitting at a picnic table
turning the tree hole to parable, as tourists duck in,
as the sun sets, as the light on the bark and leaf meal
fades, as we wrap our scarves around our necks
and the hole sits pretty, waiting for us.

Portals

Headed home after Shakespeare—shipwreck of puns, everyone thinking they're someone else—only to be blocked by yellow tape of a crime scene. Man with a gun in the mountains.

Circled round to this portal—tea shop with dark Pu'erh leaves unfurling in white cups. Man with long beard, black robe pours over lotus brick, stone pots. Water steams in wooden platter.

Dark red walls with hieroglyphic scrolls, bronzed dragons. Shoeless man at a table, his things in a garbage bag, stares into our eyes. Are we characters in his story? The tea shop, like a temple, embraces him.

Couple in the corner melds beneath blue gray heron and crescent moon. The woman twirls dark hair around her finger like my sister did when she was young and lost. Cattail and lavender tattoos peek out from orange top. Her back chimes with blue inked birds on branches above.

Many couples shelter over small quiet pots. Coleman Hawkins warms the air with "Body and Soul." Teeth flash in portals, hands flutter like butterflies as stories fly out.

The watchful man's pot lid clatters in the corner. Breezes from the heatwave's last sigh slide through the door to his mind, we hope, and to mine. In my small cup, black tea that "tastes of peat and cold granite." Like concrete where too many lie. No steeped warmth, no place to go.

Yellow-taped road encircled by camps where fires were set in the forest. Tall green ribbons ripple ocean to city—fuel for the mindless match toss or angry spark at the end of its rope.

Anything can happen. Paradise lost, regained. Yesterday, a neighbor slumped over a wheel. Someone happened to see him in time, before the stroke unrooted his mind.

Nestling in time's net, unseen beside shimmering fish, until caught. Lockdown in my daughter's school. Flash of a silvery knife. Transfixing. Bright fish in the inky canyons of Monterey Bay.

Like the yellow tape. Sequins on a dress worn to Shakespeare. Tiny gold lizards in the dust. Gleaming tea strainer. Lampshade glowing on Quan Yin's head. Owl's speckled trill in the night. Quick flash of hot water over leaves in white cups. Bright moments of danger and cheer capture our eye as we swim in black water.

Thanksgiving

The gist of this spread is delicious
A table set with dishes of fire
A moonbeam walking the floating fashion
Pictures of the first feast, birds and corn
Grouse feathers fallen, circles on soil
Oracles the color of earth and flame.

The woman's red sweater falls off her shoulder
Just slightly and will not be converted
To the candle-lit table's rank of religion.
Tonight she summons all the old things
Inside the ice box, in the hands of guests
Things that have a bit of yeast or taste
A bit like wine. She will not throw them out tonight.

Her mind is a chase of memories.
Curled fronds of tobacco and rich yellow dirt.
The trampling of buckled feet on the shore.
Black hats kindle the ice-cut air, give height
To breeches planted in the field.
A ring of ashes, a ring of flame smolder
Around the forks. Behind, in the forest,
Smudge sticks burn to ash. No ceremonial
Blackening on foreheads as heaven consumes
The smoke.

Giving her shoulder white as the oval
Faces that flicker around the candle.
Shadows gather and slip. Dance in the hollows
Of skin. Her mouth burning, she shapes
The word.

Smoke Progressions

Lamp burns above a book in whose pages
    of smoke burn cities of words.
  Lift this spoon to my lips with no history
        lingering upon this tiny shovel.
   Stripped and glazed to a reflection,
      between my parted lips, a trap of confession.

Lift veils of smoke to feed. What is
   underneath, uncounted? Lips unmoving
     chant in the dark the practical ave echoed
in larger hallways than you can imagine.
       Follow the infatuation of architecture
   and dream it loose from the starving question.

Outside the cathedral, a flower cart. Woman
      of smoke and perfume. Pale fingers curl
    around violet stems. White taper grays to nub.
       Knuckles sprout smoke. She chants

Love, you love me like smoke
   round the lips, never quite requite.
  A light is presumed in the hinge of wrist.
      Slip back in, a snake looting
the house, sun unclenched and redolent
     between your knees. The next night
a theme. Something diminishes.

      Collapsing your silken robe in the corner
  where from a window flowers spill.
Lamp burns above a book in whose pages
   of smoke burn cities of words.

Driving that Road to New York to See You

Lights dissolve an oily moon black netted
in Catskill branches. House lights spark, flush
from this touchwood desire as I divide memory
into this slick hour. Your absence falling

away by thin shades or sheets that fall off
us when shoulder blades shine wet fins. Small
of your back is a fire in the hollow
of belly, curved hips, bones. Driving this bend

I imagine your small white room in Soho
opening a peony in dark garden
soil. City of decomposed dreams, spare parts
of despair. Woman on the corner

with spaghetti can of bills and coins.
Nights where every eye is hunger, your eyes
search for keys, fumble at the lock and
someone hisses sssugar behind your neck,

and fear's gray fingers jerk you up six floors
to your small white room. Window
shuttered among hives of brick and glass
most nights open to electric Cafe

Borgio and cones of streetlight rain.
Swells of laughter, a group singing parts
from the opening at La Mama.
My tires crack time over Fishs Eddy bridge

as I remember walking into Prince Street.
Boots on cracked sidewalk worn round as river rocks.
Our ribs touch in this dirty rain. Glance down
quick to miss rivulets of soda and piss,

but our eyes do not veer for long, each second
clearing out a separate space to stand.

Fingers burn. A woman sells gloves on a
street corner table. She smiles. As we sift

through her warm gloves maybe she knows we're in love.
Signs of winter approach: tunnel gusts and
autumn coats flutter out like sail canvas
around craning masts. Where does she sell

in December? I know I will remember
her eyes flashing. We choose black angora,
$10, thank her, enter the subway at 23rd.
I know I will remember her eyes. Flashing.

Many bare hands. I pull these images
through a slipknot, cross George Washington Bridge.
Lights flicker fire in the island. A red
capillary pulses on the map.

Your window opens a steady eye.

Both And

Clad in your shirt of chaos, you arrive,
driven to the edge: Provincetown, tip
of the boot kicked out to sea. You bring wine,
paints in your tackle box, canvas and time.
Bouquet of brushes swept and tossed upon the bed.
Like old times, the cottage will be filled.

My partner's departure yesterday exploded
like a hot dish, left me waving. Today,
old friend, I gaze at your unpacked bags:
weatherproof, punctureproof, fireproof.
Fire. We are selling off everyone else
for this. That edge we define as the lapse
from questions, a natural marriage of wit
and wonder. But always the question if motion
or breath would plumb the depths. If both
is ever better or possible in anything.
We unite. Along the road of this spine.
We pull ourselves up bone by bone
and through the hollows.

Later we wedge a beach canvas. Paint
the curve of shoulder insinuated in amber.
Suspended Doric column, oyster and grainy.
Arms extend to brushes. We title this "Both And."

The cottage. Seems I'm immutable cradled
in your palm. But as with seasons and everything,
there will be a return and a shedding:
home, vows sworn among backyard roses.
Small domes of blood on fingertips.
There was a need this strong, could transmute
a feast of bushes, leave a half empty bottle,
clear green in the window?

Outside, small moon hidden
behind the lighthouse. Light
missing from the sky.

Mist off the ocean, dry ice
would lick the skin off your bones
like a dog's rough tongue.
Don't worry about the paths of light
that expose the true density of mist
sweeping into it over and over
like a scythe through smoke.
Tonight, vision missing from its shore.
No clues but under the waves.
There the light is forever the smoky light.
Plum, the color of maybe.

Painting by Porchlight

Liturgy: this my shrine
of brushes, rats, and prayers.

The wharf rat crept past same
acacia twice tonight. Big as
a baby, it fixed its burning
eyes upon my canvas.

In dim light sizzling gnats
I await some sign, a jingle
of your keys, when

cats leap. Scatterdust.
Too big this constant rat.
I shake a banishing stick.
Again swap stick for brush.

Our future feels still as dust.
Two years we lay in waiting
til bones so dry would spark
from the least rub of warmth.

This portrait was born in fire.
A finishing piece I name "Both And,"
a flame unsnuffed by midnight fog, nor
the absence of your footsteps on the walk.

Now it seems you take your turn
in the bushes, beach, and moon.
A serpent to every rat.

A car. Voices. Footsteps.
You rustle to the porch,
eyes gleam.

Seawall

Hired to patch a sea wall, you and I
always gathered mud to repair others' walls
whenever we threatened to crumble,
fastening them against monsoon.
Her wall was next to Dos Passos' house.
With her weary air of the classic past, she
descended the stairs in caftan to talk about
all the changes and watch us plug her wall.
Hours passed under the sun. She pointed out
where O'Neill's theater was torn down.
Mailer's—the only brick house in Provincetown.
Silent, we spread white patches on gray rock.

You scooped the last mortar before it stiffened
in the pail. Mixed more, stirring fast.
Cement fine as flour, like pollen to breathe.
And the water swayed closer to the seawall.
In the unfilled cracks nestled delicate crabs.
We relocated them to the dock, then layered
cement, sand, and seaweed in chasms,
galling, smoothing, inserting chips
of broken china. Giant gray stones
flickered in the sun.

When she retreated with her golden retrievers,
you said we could never return to this place.
I brought water, stirred the hardening dust.
Sun setting, high tide closing in, we
washed the shards.

Waiting It Out

In this perfect middle, an edge of pull
in both directions. The center saying
it would like to hold, would like to but
these conversations tighten the knot of
I am calling to say I am in your peripheral
sight like moths afraid of light. A yes
that informs the no, too soon, too informed
with what we cannot possibly know.
I reach attempting definition of pulls
that imply the falling away. Name strands
that tug tighter this knot. It could break,
unraveling relief or something like death.
She is gone and she and she, all leaving
until what is left but leaves
in a wind so free the strength of a tree
is needed, one rooted so far it will not budge
but give answers in how far it sways,
looks lithe through all this gust.
Oh rain sadness, your many departures
ensure the unexpected returns.
She is gone and she and she.

Rummage

Apart from three or four things I wouldn't
have said if you paid me, there's nothing I'd
take away from that last apartment we shouldn't
have stayed in. Together so long, apartheid
seemed only diplomatic, but compromising.
Splitting leases, cats, and furniture like
hairs seemed less Socratic than synthesizing
all our woes and listing, with plants and bikes
in one estate sale price: EVERYTHING MUST
GO! The squabbles and winces, the dish-
set and spices, the mower, the spite, the trust
and niceties. ALL! Nothing can stay. Wish
you had the leather, the fast wit, the cool chain
and ball? Sorry. Buy one, you take them all.

Differentia

I.
Late nights, fan whirs ripples through our sheets.
Blackberries fall on fresh-mown blades
straining through clay. Loon fetches nest-things
as the lake turns in its sleep. Tomorrow,
the only sounds—hollow ring of cut pine
stacked against the edge of solitude.

II.
Last week we drove to the other edge of extremes,
everything above surface, buildings hatched
from the granite island knocked against the scant
Manhattan sky. Long coil of multicolored steel
tunneled and bridged itself in the opposite direction.
We are blessed with timing sometimes,
though we lose track of the whole concept
in the freezing or the melting remote.

Just above the black-pocked sidewalks we float,
dirty angels happening upon an opening
at the Angelika: girls in midriffs and platforms,
retro baby dolls with yellow-stained fingers
tapering to brilliant ashes play it cool in front
of camera crews who hustle fresh reviews
of civilization falling, again. Articulate street talk,
they drop into each others' sentences
like coins in a slot machine. I dig for matches
at the sight of an old man's unlit
cigar he'd clearly rather chew. I forget old needs.

Jazz or chronic fatigue await us
around every corner. Calisthenics of buildings
thrust smokey heads into thick blue.
My head, a fog of nerves, as I blitz through love
and fear. Faces enforce this pedestrian
oscillation but sometimes, turning a corner,
they come together (awe): beneath

black gridwork, lined faces of worried windows.
Flash of artist's hand, furrowed face,
draws blueprint for Soho apartment long ago.

In this smoke-bitten sky, the only demands
live outside, or just upon, the skin. We turn
the corner, walk into the wind.
Coffee, music, and smoke assault. Always
a traffic of words, producing or consuming.

III.
I write an "Ode to the City when I am Not There":
bad coffee and dour faces in upstate.
Out these half-lidded windows, gaunt faces
of shedding trees keep me company.
O'Hara keeps me company too, but he sighs
a lot and can't wake up here, miles
from anywhere, no matter how many cups I pour.
No enthusiastic sandwiches and "hum-colored
sidewalks" to run off to. Even lunch, an occasion
for odes when you step into such dissonant
music. O solitude, when I consider the claustrophobia
on the granite island—16 million stacked 7 high
per square yard—I too sigh. Here it's the wind
like a stream of cars on the Henry Hudson.
Things are what they are. Everything stays
put. People stay put, grow old, die.

Autumn lingers anxiously. Green leaves
and their illusion of progress will be
struck down by quick frosts whose work will be
seen in a scatter of history within the week.
A miasma of dying yellow weeds, split-stocked
and crying absorbs the gaze. We are
pulled to the center of this last stand against winter,
a rare thickness preceding stubble we tolerate.
Judgements against nature futile. Brief entr'actes
to collect our arsenal of impressions.

Change does occur here if you observe it in a certain
light. Holding on, we utter untimely dreams
as earth speeds elliptically away from the sun. A cold wind
guards us against sleeping through one more year.

If You Spoke

And so in the fields where crows
Eyed our flashing silver rings,
Flinging light as we talked,
Walked arm in arm in light
Too big for our small footsteps
Insinuated in the field's tight ruts.

The nothing to say that wasn't said
And the nothing that was.

A snowfall would have cleared
Things up. As it was, a sponge
Of mud over our toes, buried
In little graves, digging as we
Walked. No pressure to undermine,
But to mine the underworld of thoughts
Unspoken, unspeakable.

I imagined your voice if you spoke
Would crack and your adolescent
Fears would emerge, all bad luck
Fluttering out like dark moths
From cracks we took care
Not to step on just yet.
In the trees, crows listened
To our silent fears.

Never too early to go home.

How Did We Find Each Other?

And who are we, we asked after years
slipped by without remembering our origin
story or if we should worship it as others
before tended to do. Just because we happened
to bump into each other hard and stuck there,
should we run a three-legged race through time?

These are all good questions, but we're not
invited to ask them in present company
without causing a rush for the door.

I see a continuum of qualities when I look at you
and sometimes even myself, though I know my
own interruptions well enough, what a pile of fictions
I've become. Almost by accident. There was the era
of the cowboy hat, another of Lacan, of meditating
on emptiness, still another of forgetting what I came
here to do which I seem to be doing now but not
particularly well. These all could have happened or not.
Then there was you, your face coming at me like an old
home movie flickering light and dark, slowing down
long enough to make a choice.

And here we are, wondering how do we find each other
and who were we. Deep in the cave now with our eyes
adjusted to the light knowing its source is behind us
somewhere or, if we're turned around, in front of us.

White Noise

Mama—irises grow so heavy this year.
   With their buttery palms they amaze.
     There is nothing left to offer
       but would stay too long.
  Nearby roses bow in prayer
     so why await
 (the crunch of the next season
underfoot is a punchline you call out
        too soon).
 Along the fence of our lovers'
   promises, a single design.
A vine, a wound.
    I am etched—
     as perennial as—
how fleeting! Three years
   felt to contain how many promises
      (suspended)—

(where then would you have—)
  where you slick off your past
      in the velvet bathroom
replace it with   nothing
 unmade, beautiful as
      the tousled bed today.
Through many rooms, doors open
      at the pace of your gaze.
 We see the unfolding,
     pressure of a thigh
     where it lay.
Corner where I would return.

Why the Song Cannot be Sung

Because the night swallowed my tongue
        and waiting was a tuneless song
                that played itself on a loop
      Because the bird flew into the clock
  and clipped its wings, its cry
      hurt the night which swallowed
          my tongue
Because reflections of screens
      stood in for your eyes,
            and I was lost unseen
  inside a clockwork of cues
Because no tears fell as I mouthed
          these words, invisible
      thoughts, like my mouth,
    grew dry, a rind in the sun
Because the ants adore the rind
           especially in the night
  when its sweetness seeps
     after clocks and boxes go dark
    And the bird without wings
sleeps in her cloister where
      her tiny dreams fly out
      into the cinema of night
          where we all must meet
on cliffs between this year
      and the next below
   wet stars

IV.

You Are a Found Object

Inland from Beyond

I meant to come here to mourn. Remember you
before the next compression of deadlines entombs
another rank year, if there is one. But I can't.
Pick up books from his shelves, as if relics. Sex
and escapism come dancing out of pages, skeletons
cocking their hips leftward then back in a Day of the Dead
dance. I dare you. Come here, sugar skull. Return
to something lost, like a neighborhood. Coltrane and
green glass warm around candles. Disco ball sparkling
in the Diamond Heights bower. Breath spinning, we'd
watch through your Castro windows, love-lengthened
on green sheets. Jasmine sparkling in the black sky breeze.

Now, on Potrero Hill, skyscrapers sprout like dreams
in a garden of words. Plum-tinged succulents, orange
poppies, yellow daisies carpet the ground. Dizzying
plenitude fragrant with a neighborhood—no, city—full
of jasmine. All day, all night. No need to stoop to smell.
It loves you by the Bayside wherever you wander.
Outside a theater, pulsing up an inclined street at midnight,
window shades open to hills that twinkle in fog's drift.

Thanatos made its calls. We made love up until the death
of my father and even after. The hot Sunday morning until
the call: a friend taken by breast cancer. This one burned
scars across all our chests. Then our cats, one by one by one.
Gregorian chants for the emotional one. Are you all waving
to me from beyond? I project onto trees and skies. Try to
bring you back, though I'm not doing such a good job.
Then Kevin Killian waved goodbye, leaving the rest of us
to hold up the skies. San Francisco won't stop crying.
I read *The Year of Magical Thinking* and hope I feel lucky.
Lit clouds move over the Mission. The fickle bright dragon
touches down on its sultry journey over us, inland from beyond.

One Place or Another

It's like the Phantom of the Opera
playing in Grace Cathedral except
he's just an ordinary dramatic
San Francisco dude clad in gray
t-shirt and beard, making
the gray statuary hold their breath
as he plays wrong notes and drops
pages between songs.

Is there a rule that church organ
music must play your nerves like
dogs howling in the basement?
Don't go there, you wince, as
G sharp and A grate—dissonant
busybodies by the fence.

I feel bad. We are in the pews scribbling
"poems" while he flips through pages
playing a scary chord here, a haunting
fragment there. I am happy when he shifts
to calliope-lite. Now all is sunny in the bright
city by the Bay until he "resolves" our happiness
with notes from the afterlife—invisible C02
molecules gathering more rapidly in "heaven"
than we dare know. All our names who smoked
up the world on *that* ledger: one big carbon sink
below us. Good use to put our bones to
and the salty regret we pack as we get ready for
our trip to one place or another.

You Are a Found Object

Between abutilon and magnolia, looms
a glimpse of the Salesforce skyscraper,
like a found object in the Potrero garden.
Temple to Vertical and Vertigo,
Brashness and Bullit. An upside-down,
unclicked ball-point poking the fog
without lyrical compense. That'll come
when it leans, giving the skyline its perpetual
precarity and nudge of mirligoes. What?

Let's all build up and up on shifting sand.
Is this a betting game? Looks safe
with its translucent periwinkle condom.
Almost scientific. But more like a monument
to Unsustainability. The Age of Technology
Ignoring Itself, replacing the groundlings
with reach and wow.

We wonder, as we peek at the empty blue
between lucky bamboo and palm, what else
they will infill. Some things remain empty.
I'm like that rusty planter, you said,
a found object with cool spirals tucked
amongst everyone, waiting for the right
blooms to be thrust into all that potential.
"I've been standing here rusting
for the longest time," it seems to smile.
The rust builds a sense of story unrushed
to tell itself but cool with the curiosity
of the watchful, planting its reflections
into the light air around the garden as it
takes shape in its eternal Sunday—
industrious, free.

Synthetic Realism, or Myths about the Fall

That's what I like about Modernism:
Between the legs of autumn crickets,
the tail light of a plane blinks.
*

If I placed my water bottle on Potrero Hill,
would the wilderness rise up to it?
*

What I like about fall air: it's a blind symphony,
a hard pear. The night is an invisible tuning fork,
center of a smoke ring.
*

Next door, a tree of crows peck the eyes
of the sun. Shuffling a deck of gold strange
words, they predict the Dow will plunge.
*

Witches are really misspelled adverbs.
*

An urgent crow flies north, his beak pulls
a thread, unravels a pale blue canopy.
*

Four yellow cranes on a black and red steamer,
bright metal necks split the sky in two.
*

Two strapping crows attached to two ideas of heaven.
*

I will never wander far from your side.
*

What will pass has passed before, but we will have
a witness, thus memory, thus song.
This idea lasts as long as we do, or maybe longer.
*

Into the bonfire goes the last page of the unwritten
book, the orchards of the past.

Storm Trilogy

Red

Tornado warning.
On a bandaged hilltop, graves.
Tangle of apple blossom
on the chain link fence.
A pink sheet of laundry
on my back is slung: it glows
a petal in a planetarium.
Rose branches then white in turn are lit.
Delicate. Astrids flash loose.
Angels are red leaves
leaping.

Blue

Shades of bruise. So heavy!
One drop and the whole bag
would split, drop a century
of slippery dimes, cheap, cheaper,
enough for all I never called,
whose unspent words are now
God's tongues all talking at once.
I could pull this big stick
from the graveyard tree.
The rain might speak softly,
But probably pour. Silver-plated-
mouth-of-the-sky pop open spraying
Teddy's dimes.

Yellow

It hides a trumpet.
Angels fly to their electrocution.
By the chainlink, my socks uncoil,
little snakes or prophets. Under
stones live beloved bones.

Then, bruise breaks
stems snap, sent to the fence
in a fury of fat yellow hands.
The townies are scattering
and popping umbrellas
like barbiturates. I am better
than Johnny Appleseed with my bag
of perfectly folded lingerie,
ready when the earth splits
to drop in.

Crooked Heart

Charles Simic died last week.
He taught me how to turn a dime
into a century, a branch into a slot
machine handle, and to be quiet
about my life and its long lines.
Or he tried.

He turned Cornell boxes into poems.
I entered one. Inside, objects or songs.
A letter opener carved by a man who
looks like a gnome in the kitsch-sprinkled
backyard of my childhood best friend.

In the center of the letter opener,
a crooked heart. Here, Simic would
veer into the black cat that ate a mouse
in front of your mother who hated cats.
The cat meant to offer a gift.

The manly gnome married my friend's
mother. A butcher retired into his
woodwork. Carved into the wooden
handle is where the heart used to be.
A chunk that fell onto the floor.

In my box of objects, stuck in
an eternal arrangement for now,
a rose quartz laid upon the hearts
of beloved dead, a broken pocket watch
engraved with my father's name.
Three pencils, one letter opener,
one stone make a song.

There to Protect the Song

First, listen to the birds.
Next, figure out which birds.
Surrounded, in the morning,
"numerous as sound" yet
punctuated by particularity.
That ringing in the deep bones
of childhood? American robin.
That long distant trill like Coltrane,
punching in when it matters?
Flycatcher. Was he ever.
And like the backup doo wop
here and gone, here and gone,
Chestnut Chickadee. Dark-eyed
Junco struts in, Pygmy nuthatch
goes nuts. Everyone on their own
perch taking in the difference. Even
my dog, yapping, gets his solos
til whisked off stage by the doorman
who is there to protect the song.

Vagrant Hummingbird

In fact, I *have* wished I could arrive at
the party like a blur of joy,
upright with purpose, my scarved neck
fuchsia with insouciant sparkle,
my cape emerald like I planned this
entrance, a cloud of wings sporting me
from feeder to flower where I
converse with color and sup
with perfect posture, then disappear
like a buzz of intention to who-knows-where,
only to return when you least expect
but most need the speed.
Even the squirrels seem lumbering
and depressed when I alight
in the middle of this awkward garden,
greenery and statuary waiting for
the spectacle, the dazzle of hope
in our still-life arrangements,
with eyes pinned to an uncertain future.

The Music that Never Ends

A painting of upside-down trees, boulders
scintillating on the surface of slow river,
as if somebody dipped their hand
into a Cezanne, set its blocks of pale green
and rosy sand in motion. Random dragonflies
alight, setting contrapuntal circles
next to shimmering blocks.

My friends lie on the sand, their bodies,
two parallel question marks clad in forest
green and plum. Other friends sway in hammocks
relishing the still river. There is sleep, and there is
writing. There is rocking, and there is release
from all worries of last night's elevated heart enzymes
and trip to the E.R. "I am just open to whatever this is,"
you said with your rippling smile, on the sandy bank.

I'm glad you are sleeping now by your calm friend.
The watchful crow's cries blend with mourning dove.
You rise up from your nap, see us writing, break
into delighted smile before turning to the Arts
section of the Times. Reflections of thin branches
look like roots that plumb the water's depths.
Crow slices above the perfect assemblage as if
to remind us that movement is without and within.

Each bird song like inner music folded out into a field
of sounds, riffle of water downstream, dogs
in the distance, sweaters moving against blankets,
everyone waking a little to the music that never ends.

Desire Blows the Dust off the World

until the bomb starts ticking and I
      notice how hot my socks are
on this day without the fog I came
      to crave, or not so much
crave, as create, but not in the right
      places like the sky, low
where it belongs, hovering over
      the beach town rather than high,
in my head, in that place where I channel
      voices, too often mine,
that create a fog of wishing for something
      other than what is. But what
is really? And is it covered up by dust?
      Underneath it all, they say,
is desire and its opposite. Tennessee
      Williams, well Blanche really,
said death is the opposite of desire.
      Bummer. Others say emptiness,
and you need to have desire to be emptied
      of it. And boy do I. This is not
something that I really want to talk about
      with all of you, whoever you are,
but I am falling forward now like a tumble-
      weed, part of some momentum,
and now I'm covered with it. But I blew
      the dust off within a day just
thinking of you. And here I am
      willing to be a honeycomb,
a reed, a stalk of beach grass,
      anything with enough wind
to blow through, to break out
      into accidental song.

Acknowledgments

Thank you to the editors of the following journals who published versions of poems in this book:

"Both And" and "Driving that Road to New York to See You": *The Ithaca Women's Anthology*
"Desert": *New Mexico Humanities Review*
"Name Outlasting Name": *The Seneca Review*
"Pumpjacks": *Puerto Del Sol*
"Thanksgiving": *Black Warrior Review* (winner of an AWP Intro Award)
Portions of "The Songs That Objects Would Sing": *Viz. Inter-Arts: Interventions*
"Zig Zag," "There's a Ruin Inside of Everything," and "The Aftermath of Future": *phren-Z*

Deep gratitude to many collaborators who have inspired me to write or who have given me valuable advice in the construction and editing of this manuscript, including my poetry group: Charles Atkinson, Terri Drake, Dion Farquhar, Farnaz Fatemi, Chopsy Gutt, Maggie Paul, David Swanger, and Robert Sward. Thanks to editors extraordinaire Nicole Heinrich and Laura Perkins and to C.S. Giscombe and Mark Scroggins for poetic camaraderie from Cornell on. Thank you to friends for the generosity of refuge: Billy Best's home in Cherokee Park, CO. made the fire poems possible during evacuation. Jim Van Buskirk's home and Allen Sawyer's garden in San Francisco enabled the writing of countless other poems.

Thank you to Marcia Quackenbush for her artful photographs; Mary Gilliana for the great cover design of this and my other books; and a loving thank you to my sister Sky Power for her painting, *Passing Through*, 2022 on the cover, and a lifetime of collaboration. I'm grateful to publisher Leah Huete de Maines and editor Christen Kincaid for their support of my book.

Most especially, thank you to my family, Laura and Emma, for your love and support throughout this project, and many others, over the years.

Biography

Roxi Power is a poet, performer, and publisher who was born in West Texas and raised in Wyoming. She received her MFA in Poetry at Cornell University. For 25 years, Power has taught at the University of California, Santa Cruz where she edits and publishes a trans-genre anthology series, *Viz. Inter-Arts*, that features recombinant forms of writing, performance, and art. The first edition, Event, won an Independent Publishing Book Award (IPPY).

Her poetry and writing has been widely published in journals and anthologies, including *Black Warrior Review* (for an AWP Intro Award); *Puerto del Sol; New Mexico Humanities Review; Prism International; Peregrine: Amherst Writers and Artists; American Book Review; Impossible to Hold: Women and Culture in the 1960s* (NYU Press); *War and Peace* (O Books): *The Book: 101 Definitions* (Anteism); etc.

Power has written and performed several Live Film Narration ("Neo-Benshi") scripts. The Benshi was the film teller in Japan and Korea during the Silent Film era, narrating and ventriloquizing the action of silent films before the "talkies." In Neo-Benshi, a form innovated by San Francisco poets in the early 2000s, films are repurposed with new dialogue performed live. She has performed Neo-Benshi at the New Orleans Poetry Festival, the Provincetown Tennessee Williams Festival, Roy and Edna Disney Theater at CalArts in Los Angeles, Yerba Buena Center for the Arts in San Francisco, Saint Mark's Poetry Project in New York, and elsewhere.

As a frequent collaborator with other artists, she has organized multiple Trans-Genre Cabarets around the country, curated the "Poetry and the Inter-Arts" Series at UC Santa Cruz, and performed original music with bands such as Mobius Operandi. She is a podcaster for The Hive Poetry Collective.

Power has been a longtime labor activist and statewide leader with the UC-American Federation of Teachers representing Lecturers at the University of California.

She lives in the redwood forest in Felton, CA with her partner, Laura Perkins, their daughter, Emma Power-Perkins, and their dogs.

www.ingramcontent.com/pod-product-compliance
Lightning Source LLC
Chambersburg PA
CBHW020336170426
43200CB00006B/408